D1795238

067411461

Ashamed or Embarrassed Is Not An Excuse

Michael Dean

Published by

MELROSE BOOKS

An Imprint of Melrose Press Limited
St Thomas Place, Ely
Cambridgeshire
CB7 4GG, UK
www.melrosebooks.com

FIRST EDITION

Copyright © Michael Dean 2006

The Author asserts his moral right to
be identified as the author of this work

Cover designed by *Maddie*

ISBN   978 1 905226 81 8

Printed and bound in Great Britain by:
CPI Bath, Lower Bristol Road,
Bath, BA2 3BL, UK

Contents

Contents

Introduction

I have anguished over this book for many years, but the more I watch the television the angrier I become. During and after each general election the future prime minister will stand up and make promises they know they cannot achieve; the promises sound good. More money for education, but the reality is that money is shaved off the lump as it works its way through the system, so when it reaches the school the lump has dwindled down so much that you will not see any changes i.e. the school overspent the year before so that money has to be returned. I came through the education system in the sixties with teacher shortages, money shortages, and for sure nothing has changed. If parents go into the school and complain their child is bullied the answer will be, "Not in this school, but we will watch the child carefully." But who will look out for that child? No one, because they have no resources spare. Also bullying is not always physically hurting a person, normally it is verbal, mind games. The story will start before my birth so that you can make your own judgment,

5

but please remember without a computer or a thesaurus spell check I would have never been able to have written this story. But it needs to be told to stop people like myself being ignored and instead get the help they need.

Chapter One

Meet the Family

My family is surrounded by mysteries; children are seen and not heard, was the rule. But I feel cheated, perhaps another member of the family suffered as I am, with reading and writing problems. I will never know.

Father was on leave from the navy, and on a boys' night out at the local picture house with his best mate they started to small talk with the usherettes, and agreed to meet up later that evening. They saw one another for sometime and married in March 1949.

My father's father was a well-built upright man who was proud of being a fireman in the local town. He worked for the Gas Board repairing gas mains in the local area. Unfortunately he contracted cancer in his later life, and he lost part of his lung at Harefield Hospital. I was allowed to visit once or twice, but my parents never explained at the time about his illness.

My father's mother was short and stooped over. I only have one recollection of her. We travelled on a bus to visit her, as we stepped into the kitchen she came through from the hallway and greeted us, and asked my sister to run an errand for her to the local shop. They also had one other son who served in the army.

My mother's father came from Reading; his parents lived on a barge on the Kennett, which never ever came up in conversation. His hand skills were phenomenal, but he was a very fiery person, who boxed for his ship whilst in the navy and won medals. My recollections of him: a placid, gentle person who would help anyone. He worked for a local building company as a painter decorator. Unfortunately he contracted cancer soon after he retired, which was not talked about like it should have been, so when I visited him, I had to walk out. I was devastated.

My mother's mother apparently came from a family with money: I never heard a word spoken about her family. It was said that she never had enough money for her burial.

Father was a well-motivated man, who had a mixture of jobs between leaving school and joining the navy: painter/decorator and removals, for sure the navy never left him. It will drive him for the rest of his days; it took 39 years before I actually stood up to him and walked out of their house and never returned. But I did tell him I wouldn't be back. He was always right; to apologise is a weakness. I grew up in fear of him. He liked his drink, but that is navy life: they never lose that.

Mother was a placid person: she worked as an usherette and at the brush factory. She was so placid I don't think she ever challenged him about anything.

They set up home together in a rural town in Buckinghamshire, which is now classed as the Chiltern Hills, they had a small bedsit, which didn't really work out for them: neighbour problems. He rode his bicycle to Bovingdon airfield everyday: "Bovingdon was built as a British Airfield, in 1941/42 but the Americans actually took it over, and the famous Memphis Bell flew from there." He rode through a village called Leyhill, where he met a work colleague. A code system was devised, so they knew if they had missed one another: a stone on the kerbstone or a chalk mark. I understand that his job was fireman/first aid. He stayed at the airfield until the Americans moved out around the sixties, at that time Heathrow was about to open and he was offered a post there but he decided to stay local and join a distributor of hardware, just outside of town.

The airfield closed down totally in 1972, and some of the land reverted back to arable farming.

My sister was in born September 1951, they moved into a larger property a few hundred yards down the road, which was still in close proximity to the school.

Chapter Two

The Right Environment

The housing shortage caused big problems for young couples, but they were more adaptable. Sharing with families was more acceptable as an option but they also kept looking, not waiting for a property to come for rent or buy.

My sister attended the local infant school, which I understand she hated as most children do. Apparently she didn't like the afternoon sleep; perhaps insecurity was the problem as I am sure both of my parents worked and she spent a lot of time with Grandma.

The local council addressed the housing problem as fast as they could. By 1955 a planning notification appeared in the local paper plus notification for redirection of footpaths; tenders were also asked for. The estate consisted of around fifty houses and thirty flats and was to be called Hivings Hill estate. "Apparently the housing estate was renamed after it was built." The estate took the shape of a 'D', the upright, all council, the inner all council, the outsides of the 'D' was private, but developed over a longer period, so by 1957 the housing estate moved on very fast and my parents were offered a house on the estate.

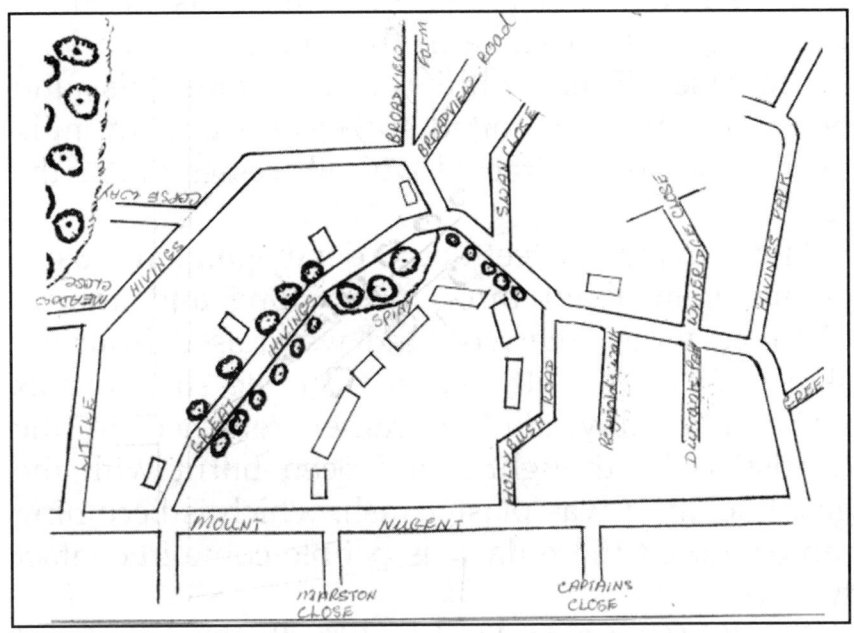

With the bus running past the door, a school 10 minutes away, playing areas for the children, but the pathway to the doors and gardens were not complete, but the tenants were allowed to move in. They had to accept the offer of a modern house, it was too good to refuse. The tenants moved in along the row, fortunately a builder moved in next door. With the excitement of new houses and the sense of community spirit a majority of tenants contacted the foreman of the site and asked if they could construct their own pathways. They were given materials and tools to carry out the build; this forged a great friendship between them.

In April 1958 I was born, unfortunately a sickly child. After six weeks I was rushed into hospital with PYLORIC STENOSIS which is virulent vomiting when a valve in the stomach is working in reverse. Then with constant tonsillitis and penicillin my teeth rotted so before I lost my milk teeth they were extracted with abscesses under the teeth.

After having my teeth out I developed a red band on my chin about three inches long and around one inch wide. The red band was raised from the skin with lots of little spots over the surface, this irritated terribly. So my father returned to the dentist as he thought I had been burnt with the gas. Luckily it was plaster rash, which is becoming more evident these days as people come in contact with pine trees.

By 1961/62 my spate of bad health was over and I started to play in the garden. Across the road they had started a new private housing development with around 20 semi-detached houses. One glorious day I was playing in the garden already to go and visit Grandma and the gate was mistakenly left open. Not knowing any different I walked through. There stood in front of me a big hedge, to my left a pathway and to my right were two circular tar macadam areas for children to play. I walked to the left where there was a hole through the hedge. My father parked his car on the other side, so down the slope into the road and a big wide open space: a building site. Of cause nobody was working, so I started to climb on a stack of bricks. In those days there was no such thing as pallet deliveries, everything was handball. The bricks where delivered by lorry and stacked by hand which left like walkways one brick width right along the stack. Of course I climbed up but part-way along the stack everything went black.

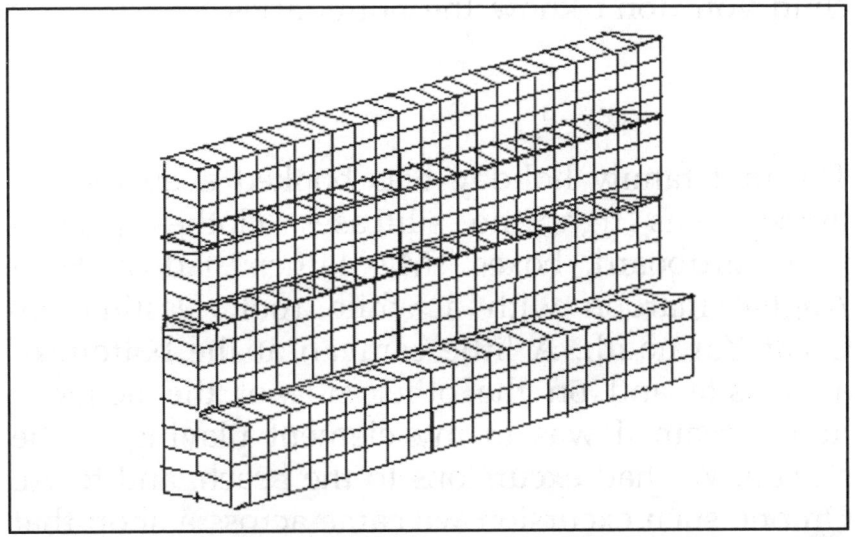

The next thing I remember, I am in the kitchen with my father shouting at me, blood over my face, down my white cardigan, the outing to Granny's cancelled, but the funniest thing they never took me to hospital, that would cause embarrassment and that is not acceptable, so the scars I carry on my head are 25mm x 2mm & 20mm x 4mm and they should be a thin silver line. People from this era where raised to be hard, don't complain; stop making a fuss, that's only a cold. I am afraid that I was brought up under that umbrella; children are seen and not heard. Any visitor to our house, or if we visited anybody, we sat in a chair and didn't move and didn't speak unless we were spoken to. The problem with that is it never leaves you, studying people becomes a habit, so learning is more difficult because you cannot ask questions, or put your hand up in class for fear of being shouted at or threatened. This is a very fine line but as a child you don't know the boundaries.

The first family holiday was booked even though money was tight; no suitcases, clothes packed into cardboard boxes. My father had a Ford Anglia; maroon with a white roof. Destination: Great Yarmouth. A little caravan at the bottom of a big site and on the other side of the hedge a little stream; I was in my element playing in the stream. We had excursions to the beach, and town. On one such excursion we came across a shop that took pictures with a monkey. I was too afraid to hold the monkey so we moved on to a shop that rolled rock. You could actually see them building the rock up with the letters and colours so when they rolled the finished thing out it grew and grew so several people took part in the rolling process. They kept trimming the length so they could keep it on the table. The process carried on until the rock was the same circumference as a bottle top, then they cut the length. We then backtracked up the high street and after a lot of convincing I had my picture taken with the monkey. Teeth missing, hair sticking up and a monkey on my arm. They thought it was lovely, but that's parents.

Unfortunately they ran out of money mid-week so everything went back into their boxes and the journey home was taken. I've always wondered if the blame lies with me for the shortened holiday.

With the car shopping trips to Hemel Hempstead market happened every Saturday as a routine. Fruit and vegetables first and back to the car, then father's Brylcreem which came in a log; sachets like you would buy sausage meat today. Woolworths was the next stop for broken biscuits. "Apparently they lost me in Woolworths one Saturday and I ran outside crying." He didn't like that as it was embarrassing, but this happens to lots of children sometime in their life.

Down the High Street we would walk to the London shop. Mother called it that because it was full of gadgets like lava lamps. I used to carry on to the butchers where they had live eels in a galvanised tank and they swam around and around. They also had chickens on a spit roast in the window which you see in most supermarkets today, also you would see them in a fish and chip shop; that was 43 years ago.

We would then travel back to Bovingdon to the bakers, which had been in that village for 40 years. The bread was very good but as soon as we got home we had to have a roll and a cup of tea.

Chapter Three

Starting School

By September 1963 I had no recurrences of sickness and was fully recovered. It was time to start school. My sister can always remember being in assembly on the first day of term and a commotion started in the entrance hall, which interrupted the morning assembly. To her shock and horror the headmaster walked through the hall with me on his shoulder screaming and kicking; she bowed her head in shame. I was taken to the classroom and introduced to my teacher, Mrs Fletcher, a lovely lady. Nothing was too much trouble, with painting easels and a shoe-shaped piece of wood with holes to teach us how to tie up your shoes, Janet and John reading books. Even though she was a patient lady, I am afraid that learning for me was very difficult and as an individual the class moved on. So-called individuals like myself are just left behind, until it was realized that there were more children in the class failing, and then hurriedly a special reading group was structured in the library. A cheap exercise to make people think they were addressing the problem, but if you are failing in reading there must be other areas that need addressing: mathematics and writing skills.

So everyday my sister dragged me to school with my parents thinking their son was progressing, with the school blaming the child for being slow, so the child's best interests are not being addressed.

The problem is the teacher is not allowed to speak on the child's behalf. This will come more apparent as we go along.

BUCKINGHAMSHIRE EDUCATION COMMITTEE

Headmaster:
R. Fisher
—
Phone: Chesham 470

The Durrant C.P. School,
Pond Park,
Chesham,
Bucks.

July 1964

Michael has made very slow progress in
reading and number. He tries very
hard and always gives of his best.
He enjoys group activities and always
has some interesting news to tell.
He is helpful in the classroom.

M. Fletcher.   R Fisher.

Headmaster

The evidence in the reports only brought hardship onto myself, telling me to buck up my ideas, nothing constructive, like listening to me reading.

Dramatic changes to the landscape were taking place in front of our house; the hazel hedge grubbed out, which exposed the entrance of the farm, and a smallholding. My father rented part of a building on the smallholding to park his car which had a tarpaulin across the back to keep out the driving weather.

The farm used to be a working slaughterhouse; there were no tell-tale signs or smells although occasionally you would hear a lorry go passed; I understand the slaughterhouse closed in the early 60s.

The grubbed out spoil from in front of our house was disposed of across the road at the farm. The lorries where like dinky toys compared to today's trucks; back and forth all day long the trucks worked. The drivers started to recognize that the children were local so they started to give trips to the farm with the spoil; in those days the worry of strangers was nearly non-existent so we climbed aboard. A traffic journey down a narrow lane through the farm yard and down a narrow track to the site. Of course we stayed in the truck while the tailgate was unhooked and tipped out the spoil next to a big hole. I was having a great time but unfortunately that wasn't the view of my mother, the atmosphere you could cut with a knife especially with my father; luckily the rule of the house, I had to be in bed before he came home, never allowed to see father at night whatever time.

So the summer holidays became boring, watching the other children enjoying themselves in the lorries. Taunting me was the next trick; but mother said you don't want to play with those kids anyway; but being different was worse.

With the new term approaching a shopping trip was required to our local town because chain stores and shopping malls were non-existent. The local male outfitters were the only places; all of the wares were kept in display cabinets and angled drawer cabinets on the wall which pulled out so that the wares could be seen. All of your measurements were required before a sale took place, nothing was left to chance.

That dreaded September day came around and I was dragged to school again; and they did have to drag me, I always felt that they would get me to school and move, but nothing like this ever happened; probably just timidity, that is how my parents interpreted the situation, they must have loved me but they would never show it.

I could never relax in the classroom at school: school should be enjoyed and this would actually make the learning process easier. The new teacher tried to help and with extra reading in the library most days looked like they were paying dividends, but creative writing turned out like a spider had crawled across the page, so I thought things are not so bad, until one particular weekend my confidence was shattered. Sitting in the sitting room on a black three-seater settee watching the television, my father came rushing from the kitchen and grabbed me accusing me of pinching money from his drawer. I must have shook like a leaf and my mouth must have dropped open. I tried to tell him that I had no idea what he was going

---

BUCKINGHAMSHIRE EDUCATION COMMITTEE

Headmaster:
R. Fisher

— 3070

Phone: Chesham 470

The Durrant C.P. School,
Pond Park,
Chesham,
Bucks.

July 1965

Michael has never found learning easy,
but he always works hard and does his
best. He has made fair progress with
his reading and writing, though he finds
number work difficult. He is a friendly,
helpful member of the class, and takes a
special interest in the nature table.

Class Teacher

Headmaster

R Fisher

---

on about, as you could imagine it was only a one-way bawl out. I heard no more about the money until I was thirty-nine when one weekend all of the family were together and he told a story about my mother giving money to a friend and hadn't told him. He never apologized when I was a child and he didn't even remember when he told the story.

In my opinion you don't treat your children or anybody else in that manner; but you must remember you never apologise because it makes you weak, so I carried this around for many years.

My brother was born on February 1965, so I was no longer in the limelight.

With a second opinion in writing to my parents the alarm bells still didn't ring. The blame was solely on my shoulders with comments such as you will have to read more. Other children's parents listened to them read but this was never an option for me.

The housing estate was growing opposite our house with building materials over a vast area. Site offices were put in the spinney 50 yards from our house, one of which was a night watchman's hut. He had a brazier in front of the door as he sat in the doorway talking to us children, with similarities to the character green grass,with the big overcoat, and beard had white hair to match.

School had returned after the summer break and

I loved to get home to play in the spinney and talk to Jasper the night watchman; that was our name for him. Then one evening he suggested that we put some potatoes in the brazier, of course I flew home and shouted to my mum, "I am taking two potatoes." I flew back to the spinney and Jasper placed the potatoes in the embers at the bottom of the brazier. Time slipped by; we were in our element. Then of course Father came home and found I was not in bed. This triggered a rage: a child of mine failing at school out at this time of night.

With my name being shouted I turned tail and ran towards home. He caught me at the edge of the spinney, took hold of my arm and dragged me home and took the Persuader from the corner and pulled down my trousers. The Persuader was a bamboo cane which was three foot long. My mother saying don't hit him and father saying you pinched the potatoes from the pantry; I just screamed and to this day don't know whether I urinated myself, the image in my mind is still vivid today.

The classroom suddenly became easier. I was asked to clean out the pigeon coop. With a chair and trowel in hand I scraped out the mess. In class they started to leave me out of lessons, reading in the library continued.

Parents' evening came around and my sister looked after me while they attended the school and went for a drink after, but he still had to give me a stern warning before he went: if there's no improvement there will be trouble boy.

The next day his tactics changed and the threat changed from karate clubs to boarding school, this frightened the life out of me; they didn't want me, came to mind. There was nothing left for me to give; my reports say to the best of his ability.

Father's Methodism caught up with him: every bill and receipt, school report, were kept in his filing system, nothing was left to chance; the report for 1966 went missing.

Occasionally you find a teacher that will speak out on behalf of the child, but they are soon pulled back into line by the headmaster. This action was taken against my father, they told him the truth. "No child of mine will attend a school for special needs, the school is failing him." The report would have been ripped up so he would never see it again to remind him of the truth that his son would always struggle through life, and he had the power to improve the situation. "Embarrassment"

As a non-achiever he would snap at me, "Read a book", "You'll be going to boarding school." I could not understand why he wouldn't listen to me read, or my mother.

I would always try my best but you always need to know the basics before you can excel. Even though I put in the effort children notice that you are failing and start ridiculing you in the playground or on the way home. To help combat this I had to join the Boys' Brigade, which met at a

Baptist church in town. Even though I attended with friend on the first occasion the joining ceremonies were daunting, and each week you worked to gain awards. I tried to enjoy the experience but you could never let your guard down for fear of being ridiculed again.

Travelling each Friday on the bus to town was lonely as my friend had dropped out of Boys' Brigade; whether their parents had no money or

---

BUCKINGHAMSHIRE EDUCATION COMMITTEE

Phone : Chesham 3070

The Durrant C.P. School,
Pond Park,
Chesham,
Bucks.

July,1967

Michael works very hard. His reading is steadily improving and he has shown progress in his mathematics, and English work. He still needs practice in handwriting, as this is very large and untidy. His patience in art and craft has resulted in the production of some very good work. He also works very hard in games and P.E.

Janet Lorkin

Class Teacher

Acting Headmistress

---

they didn't like church on a Sunday. Church was part of Boys' Brigade code so you also had a mark on your card to prove your attendance as this was also part of your achievement awards. My parents seemed happy as I attended Boys' Brigade and went to church Sundays, it probably covered up some cracks.

Our annual holiday took place at Butlins, Minehead, great fun, and the kids were contained in the camp with supervision. Trouble soon came my way as they caught me wading in mud retrieving a ball. I was marched back to the chalet, bathed, moaned at and sent back out to play, mind you, they were on holiday as well. On the Friday everything started to go back in to suitcases and packed in the car. My sister had fallen in love with a young man staying at the camp. This went down like a lead balloon. We collected her from a youth club on the site and we soon started our trip home.

A new headmaster appointed to the school caused a good many rumours; with failing school in mind, but they were so far from the truth, many children were failing. In fact it was a better option for the council: new broom clean sweep, but I am afraid it didn't help me or several others.

To build confidence into people they need to achieve goals and that is not possible by blaming the child. Where were the sociologists that are expert in this field or are they not allowed to do their job? Money is the deciding factor whether you are helped or not and the parents must agree.

Several weeks before Christmas I attended the church service. A children's play was in discussion and they approached me to play a part; I said no, but that wasn't good enough. They handed me the lines so I declined again but they would not take no as the answer, so press ganged into the play I was; telling them I couldn't read seemed to be a bad option, so I told my parents and all they could say was well done, with no offer of help. This worried me everyday but I still didn't know which way to turn. Each Sunday we practised the play and each Sunday I told them I couldn't do it; I understand why children commit suicide over bullying. As the day of the play drew near I lived in fear of the torment I would have to take from most of the school. There was no option I had to do the play. The play was an utter disaster. Monday morning the children ripped me to pieces.

Keeping out of the way was an impossibility. In the classroom and playground I copped it; rather lonely times. Luckily enough Christmas was only around the corner and they had other things to think of, and with winter nights facing them it became easier. By the New Year I only had trouble with one boy, the problem was he sat next to me in class.

Once or twice a day he would jab me in the crutch. He chose his moments very well and caught me off guard every time and this carried on for weeks. I had to tell my mother, she wanted to chase his mother down the street but this would have caused more problems and I was getting tired of keeping my head down so I managed to stop her. She could not understand why I had stopped her. I know parenthood is a challenge, but they had no idea what was happening or was it just embarrassment?

The annual holiday had a change of venue from Great Yarmouth to Westward Ho. It was more of a family holiday this time as my sister's boy friend had been invited; they travelled down in his car. The site lay back from the sea by half a mile, although it was a very interesting walk with small channels of water running through with sand eels visible if you were lucky, with a break water at the back of the beach made of round boulders which were naturally rounded as they worked their way around the head land and deposited on the beach.

Spending a great deal of time on my own as my sister was seventeen, her boyfriend twenty and my brother three. Who would want a ten year old under their feet? Half way through the first week my parents decided they were having a great time and decided to stay another week, but it soon passed. One thing I could never understand: for their two week holiday, missing school was acceptable. Illness, dentist, not acceptable to have time off school.

Summer holiday just around the corner and I witnessed the first turf war with ice cream vans; even though at that age it went over my head. While playing in front of our house the sound of an ice cream van rang out. With excitement we ran indoors for money, meeting up again at the ice cream van. It was a bull-nosed Morris with large headlights and indicators on the mudguards and mirrors on the door pillars, a short dumpy van with a freezer unit in the back where he stored and cut up the ice cream blocks. He parked in a narrow road and we all queued up for our witches hat which consisted of a rocket ice-lolly with an up turned cornet on the top. Waiting our turn patiently another tune rang out, another ice cream van pulling into the same road; Mr Whippy. He drove directly at the bull-nosed Morris and smashed the indicator. The van shook with the force, verbal abuse rang out for a few minutes and Mr Whippy reversed up and drove off. The poor man was just left with his indicator in pieces. He asked us to be witnesses but this didn't mean a thing to any of us. To children this was an adventure but things could have turned out very different as children around ice cream vans is a danger zone anyway, but it was just accepted as a laugh.

During the holidays there was no mention of me failing at school only if I misbehaved the threats of the boarding school were thrown at me. This makes you more of an introvert as you are always frightened of making a mistake. Learning by your mistakes is part of the learning curve as a person who has never made a mistake has never made anything. The consequences are you build your life to keep people out, as they may hurt you. This continues all through your life, even today at the age of forty-seven I still do it. You need no friends living in your own world, I very rarely visit my brother and sister because there's no bond, whether they have, I cannot say.

Boys' Brigade did help the situation, but there again fear still ruled that experience, the fear of Chinese whispers. One morning I walked out of my bedroom across the landing to the stairs, and my sister called me into her bedroom, reproachful of me swearing in the town centre whilst I waited for Boys' Brigade to start. I denied the allegations; they would rather listen to gossip than give me the benefit of the doubt, every time. Hurdle after hurdle I climbed, travelling to and from Boys' Brigade on dark evenings. Walking the high street before the club started there was no comprehension of danger from my parents; just a man-making exercise.

Continuing Boys' Brigade did broaden my horizon although it took a lot of courage, because of the fear aspect of being ridiculed, and knowing you're on your own; like buying bags of stale buns from the bakers for 6d and scraps on your chips. Can you trust the person who told to ask or will it be another laughter session for the boys? This destroys some people.

Personal qualities

a) Co-operation

most satisfactory.

b) Perseverance

Will work steadily without being watched or pushed.

Basic Skills

a) Reading *Still a good way below the average attainment for his age.*

b) Handwriting *alternates between print script and cursive writing though he has, in fact, developed quite a good hand in joined script.*

Mathematics

a) Concepts/Tables

Poor on the whole.

b) Practical

This tends to be below standard

c) Written

A lot of basic mechanical work has been forgotten.

English

a) Spoken English *speaks very little in oral lessons.*

b) Written English

Does very well considering the reading handicap. Has good ideas at times

c) Language

much too low in this – needs to work hard to catch up

d) Spelling

Over a year behind in spelling ability.

Other Aspects of the Curriculum

Michael mixes well with whatever group he happens to be working.

GENERAL COMMENT

I cannot see that Michael will ever make the top section in the 4th year I think he is probably working up to his capacity level

CLASS TEACHER *Thos. J. Pickett*

Michael works well and keenly in my special reading group and he takes a pride in his written work. But this is well below the standard of his class, and he must

HEAD TEACHER . . . .

Michael must work at his reading. This is all important to his progress.

R. Leighton.

THE DURRANT COUNTY PRIMARY SCHOOL

REPORT FOR YEAR ENDING JULY 19th,1968

NAME

CLASS . . . . . *12* . . . . . .

*must make a greater effort next
year. E.B.Sutton.*

The excitement of the Olympics Games was soon destroyed; this was the subject for the summer term following the games with paper cuttings, good fun. Putting pen to paper was more difficult, the only thing that would come forward in my head was a big black cloud; you couldn't see through it and nothing would come through it. The more you try the worst it becomes. You could not explain that to a teacher, they would think you came from cloud cuckoo land, so sitting back hoping that 4 o'clock would hurry up was the best option, but not the right answer. I would have given anything to change the situation and writing flowed from my pen and not being looked at as not trying or giving my best.

I keep asking myself how professional people like psychologists and teachers alike can allow this sort of cruelty to carry on in the class, and condemn a child to either a life of crime or misery.

My mother had a flair for ladies' hairdressing and one of her occasional clients came from the farm across the road. They met at the local secondary school for girls, where my sister attended, with her daughters, and fortunately this opened an opportunity for me.

A group of us boys wondered down the lane towards the farm and of course the farm dog went ballistic, luckily the attention of the farmer wife was drawn to the dog barking. She hurriedly came down the side of the bungalow, not expecting a group of boys, she shouted at the dog and instantaneously John piped up, "Could I shoot my air gun on your property?" Taken back in amazement, she replied, "Who are you?" He explained that he came from the council estate at the top of the lane. We were told to wait. On her return from a discussion with her husband she replied that we could; all of that time I was trying to pluck up courage to ask for myself, in bewilderment she recognized me, saying, "Aren't you the Jones boy?" With a lump in my throat I managed to ask. Yes she said, I couldn't believe my luck; it doesn't sound much but this changed my outlook on life because I was accepted for who I was, and not slow learner Mick.

My introduction to the farm was a slow progression to start with. The occasional Saturday and Sunday with John, who had an air rifle. This soon changed when I was given an ex-army leather jerkin, down passed my knees but it felt good. The boys found out that a .22 pellet wouldn't pass through the leather; yes they soon started using me as a target. They hit my back pretty hard but never penetrated. I learned to keep things like that to myself or that would be the end of my farm days.

Again the school report caused problems: you must try harder. Still no offer of help with reading, if I tried reading myself there was no support, it was like I wasn't there. It must have made him feel better after his moaning and hoping it will go away if you turn your back on it long enough.

The final year at middle school had started and the school started to prepare us for the transition. Trips were planned for us to attend a secondary school in the area, which really opened my eyes. Twenty-one rooms plus a gymnasium: frightening. Then when we arrived back at school the rumours started; how they punish you with a cane. Not knowing your tables would lead to punishment, of course I knew no different, no brother older than me, I was hooked line and sinker. This worried me, I tried to ask my mother questions and told her what I had heard, but the best answer was: you shouldn't take any notice of those kids, all they do is cause trouble, you shouldn't mix with them either as they have got fleas and the oldest one has got yellow jaundice. I knew at this point that father would get involved and sure enough when he came home: keep away from those kids.

This treatment over the long term made me a recluse; the art of conversation is dually learned from your parents and those allowing you to mix with other adults. As children were seen and not heard this put me at a disadvantage, then choosing whom I could mix with really destroyed my chances.

Most conversation to me is a waste of time, so I say nothing, or I pick out the information I need; don't get me wrong this was driven into me, probably not knowing the consequences. Children are for ever, not for Christmas; they need to be loved and enjoyed. By pushing them away and having no time for them the problems are implanted into the next generation and so on. Hopefully I have stopped the rot, because I suffered for such a long time; people like myself have to give their best all of the time through fear of losing a job, failing the family; by not providing would absolutely devastate me.

Handcrafts were introduced into the last term; basket weaving, leatherette stitching. The desire to please my family was beyond words, with much thought I decided to craft a pouch for my father's lighter. The pouch took shape over several weeks and I thought that this would help my quest to please him and repair the damage done to me being a non–achiever. Hoping the measurements were correct I took home the pouch with a skip in my step. When I showed my mother she agreed to allow me to wait up for my father to come home.

How stupid could I have been? I wished the ground had opened and took me for ever; men do not have purses. I explained that it was for his lighter but he pushed me away. Total devastation tears filled my eyes, unfortunately my mother's sister walked in to all of the hullabaloo. This made it worse and he ripped into me again about men not having purses. My mother took me upstairs and explained that a purse should have money in it, if you give one as a gift. On my return downstairs he had to play to the crowd and ripped into me again.

Personal qualities

a) Co-operation *Michael tries hard*

b) Perseverance *and rarely relaxes effort.*

Basic Skills

a) Reading *Slow but steady progress.*

b) Handwriting

Poor. Michael has problems with joining.

Mathematics

a) Concepts/Tables

Very slow to learn tables.

b) Practical

A good practical worker who asks for help when necessary.

c) Written

Slow progress. Michael has severe difficulties.

English

a) Spoken English

Shyness prevents Michael taking more part.

b) Written English

Highly imaginative in a macabre way.

c) Language

Poor in structure. Michael must learn basic rules.

d) Spelling

Poor.

Other Aspects of the Curriculum

Michael enjoys greenhouse and animal work. He constructed a rabbit cage after costing it. Not a keen artist but an interest in modelling.

FRENCH Poor. not much interest shown in this subject.

Mireille Lipöl.

GENERAL COMMENT

Michael finds most subjects difficult and he is slow to learn. A likeable and well mannered boy popular with others. and always keen to help.

We wish him a very happy and successful future.

CLASS TEACHER P M Hill.

Michael tries hard but he has a long way to go

HEAD TEACHER ...... R. Singleton ......

THE DURRANT COUNTY PRIMARY SCHOOL

REPORT FOR YEAR ENDING JULY 18th, 1969.

NAME ▮▮▮▮▮▮▮▮

CLASS ....ß............

The showing of his command was next: bed. This was the power freak part of him coming out, he would have really had a buzz from that as there was a captive audience.

Again destroying people was quite easy for him to achieve; I wondered if he slept at night, of course he did. Perhaps these things catch up with you later in life.

The last few weeks of school really made my life hell, as contemplating a new school and new people and knowing that I would be failing even more, because all I would receive was criticism and not constructive help.

On the presentation of the last school reports more alarming stories came to the surface. Several other children where being railroaded into secondary schools who should have never been presented at these schools. One particular parent had hounded the school for months, appealing that her daughter would never cope with secondary school and a special needs school should be considered. Because the wheels of bureaucracy turn so slowly, or the head of the school could have seen pound signs over the heads of the children running around the playground, the child's needs were not considered. During the summer recess this parent was approached by the authorities saying that their daughter should be statemented which starts the processes of a child's needs, medicals, parents' views, and so on.

The real alarming part of this story was that they forced this child into secondary school for two weeks. Of course the teachers were given this information, so when the teacher addressed the new class informing them of the curriculum, she politely informed them of the individual that wouldn't be taking part as she would only be there for two weeks. She was supposedly a professional person, but the damage that she had just caused would stay with that child for the rest of her life.

The final prognoses, children who are foul-mouthed, uncontrollable, terrorize other children, or just downright disruptive, seem to be processed through the system at great speed to help that child. Surely every child should have that chance?

Chapter Four

Manipulative Paper Work

John's house was under the canopy of the spinney, four doors away, so we quite often met at the farm. His interests included motorbikes as well as shooting, and he quite often used his NSU quickly up and down the lane, which did annoy the local residents. Because of its age the maintenance was quite high and with the price of spares it could have been an expensive hobby. To keep the expenses down he went to the local motorcycle shop and took parts from scrapped cycles, which were cheaper.

Over the summer break I was drawn to the farm as well as motorbikes, great fun. Then one day John asked if I fancied a fishing trip to the aquadrome. My parents were quite adamant about me going, with no lectures, so the next day we tracked to the train station, and took the shuttle to the main line, standing there admiringly as I thought John had travelled on trains before: wrong. Of course the first train in was a through train to Harrow on the Hill. Not knowing this we piled on with all our equipment and the train moved off, station after station went passed. I became very anxious and asked John if we were close to our stop. "When the train stops we get off," he replied. Suddenly the train slowed down and stopped, then he explained that we had passed our stop and would have to go back.

We told the stationmaster what we had done. He grinned, and then started to lecture us on not leaving the station, he then took us to the platform and dared us to move. After a few minutes our train arrived, and this time stopped at our destination.

The experience of my first train travel haunted me for several weeks after so taking up fishing as a regular hobby passed me by.

The new term for school drew close, John said that he would accompany me to school the first day, I thought this would be a good idea; an old hand showing me the ropes. Thank god I did. with the vast amount of people there I didn't know which way to turn. He took me through to the assembly hall where we were split into four house groups. Penn was my designation, this then determined which classroom I should attend; but this also categorized you into your learning ability status.

All my praying for a helpful teacher paid off; a fair-haired lady around thirty with a long, distant voice. She drew on the blackboard our weekly timetable for lessons, which we had to copy. Every lesson was a change of class and a total of twenty-one classrooms, so the learning of classrooms had to be quick, as you were allowed five minutes between classes.

Luckily she waited for us stragglers to catch up before we started our grand tour of the school. We started off in the craft room, enormous room, equipped with a kiln and several potters' wheels; the library was the length of two classroom, and then onto the metal and woodwork rooms. During the tour of these rooms we were told that they didn't have a full-time teacher for these subjects, so it would be unlikely the first year would take these subjects.

The tales soon started to fly about the deputy headmaster, Mr Jones. He supposedly ruled by the cane, with a technique of pinching and twisting your stomach beforehand, then three strikes with the cane, soon put the fear of god into me.

Lessons for the first day were toned down some-what as a relaxed atmosphere and teacher intro-duction were most important. The instruction of carrying physical education equipment, and games equipment to school every day came a bit of a blow as there were no lockers and thieving was quite rife.

School meals 60p a week and first years were on the first sitting overlooked by the teacher table. The meals were quite varied: beef, cottage pie, fish

CESTREHAM COUNTY SECONDARY SCHOOL
CHESHAM

REPORT FOR THE TERM ENDING.....CHRISTMAS, 1969.....

Form ......1 P.....

No. in Form.....28.....

Form Position.....—.....

Conduct.....Excellent.....

Punctuality.....V. Good.....

Attendance.....V. Good.....

SUBJECT	SET	TERM LETTER	EXAM. %	EXAM. POS.	COMMENTS	MASTER
ENGLISH		D	30	22	Good work but careless.	E.H.
MATHEMATICS		C−	34	21/28	He works to the best of his ability.	E.W.
RELIGIOUS INSTRUCTION		D	22	16/23	This — that work read this first	J.H.
SOCIAL STUDIES		D	30	23	Shows interest. Works well.	E.H.
HISTORY						
GEOGRAPHY (French)		C	24	17/28	Has worked well.	Sh
FRENCH		C			Needs more confidence in oral work	C.H.R.
ART		D			Will improve	D.H.
CRAFT						
MUSIC		B			A good singing voice	G.H.D.
GENERAL SCIENCE		C+	26	14/28	Has produced satisfactory work in accordance with his ability	D.H.
RURAL SCIENCE		E	10	26	Can't keep anything in his mind. Quite works well	a.
TECHNICAL DRAWING						
METALWORK						
WOODWORK						
PHYSICAL EDUCATION		C−			Satisfactory	J.A.M.
DRAMA		C			Can be good - lacks confidence	S.H.S.

TERM LETTER: 'A' Very Good.   'B' Good.   'C' Satisfactory.   'D' Weak.   'E' Very Weak.

REMARKS	REMARKS
Quiet, but helpful boy. Works to the best of his ability.	Carry on making an effort
E. White Form Master.	J.J.T. Roberts Deputy Head Master. 2 5 JAN 1970
Parent's Signature.....	Next Term begins on.....

pie, steak and kidney pie, and fish and chips and all meals come with a pudding.

Very little interest shown at home about school, even though I explained about the teacher shortages. Perhaps they thought miracles might happen over the next five years, or should they intervene and cause scenes until their child did receive the special needs help. "That is for you to decide."

Plotting the classrooms in my head came fairly easily, but games and physical education were another story; after these lessons you where allowed five minutes to shower and change ready for your next lesson. No warming of the water, and with the tutor observing and counting down the minutes, failing in this quest resulted in a punishment of the offender, a whack with his training shoe.

Situations like this would appeal to my father, discipline and character building was high on the list. Make him into a man, deviation didn't exist in his vocabulary; perhaps I shouldn't blame him but he always said that you should always be responsible for your actions.

Works to the best of his ability seems to work for my father as his signature appears firmly at the bottom of the page, but no doubt he will have the last word, as he always did.

Even though I was condemned to struggle through school, happy thoughts were with my sister as her marriage was to take place in March.

Our relationship was never close due to seven years between us but this didn't mean that we didn't love each other; it just meant we had different interests. "Who wants to take their brother courting?" Also my sister is clever.

They decided to get married on a Thursday because he ran an electrical shop with his parents in the town. The discussion about me attending the wedding was very short: I had to go to school and miss the wedding. I was allowed to go to the evening reception with no extension on bed time as I had school the next day, wow.

That day is imprinted into my head; looking out of the craft room window thinking my sister's wedding ceremony is taking place at this time. I suppose that was the last word: he cannot afford time off school as he is so far behind.

Attitudes of this intensity cause many problems with the child, deep into their head goes thoughts of being rejected, beyond help, useless, but those thoughts are for life because they are driven in over years.

Luckily I found a family which didn't judge, even though one morning I crept off to the farm. On my arrival I found that they were going to treat the cattle for worms, the cattle crush was in place; this is a narrow cage, built out of tubular steal, the length just longer than a fully grown beast, a semi-circular top to stop the cattle from jumping through, one door with a sliding gismo to catch the cattle's head so that it is held in place to put a nozzle into their mouth for the drench.

CESTREHAM COUNTY SECONDARY SCHOOL
CHESHAM

REPORT FOR THE TERM ENDING........................ 17 JUL 1970

Form ......1.E.........................

No. in Form.....25......

Form Position............—.........

Conduct. Excellent..............

Punctuality. Excellent..............

Attendance. Very Good..............

SUBJECT	SET	TERM LETTER	EXAM. %	POS.	COMMENTS	MASTER
ENGLISH		C+	18½		Co-operative	9.5
MATHEMATICS		C−	49	16=/25	Good progress has been made.	EW
RELIGIOUS INSTRUCTION		D	20	19/19	His work has been deteriorating	SW
SOCIAL STUDIES		C	28		Willing to listen	9.5
HISTORY						
GEOGRAPHY		C	14	18/23	Has worked well	
FRENCH		C+	24	16	His term work is good but his examination work lets him down	CJR
ART						
CRAFT		C			Quite good at modelling.	J.B
MUSIC		Singing B+	Theory 16.	23/23 23rd	Usually good written work — away for revision hence result. Good singing	YAP.
GENERAL SCIENCE		C+	26	12/23	He works well, but his exam result is disappointing	
RURAL SCIENCE		E	26	22	A poor term's work.	PR
TECHNICAL DRAWING						
METALWORK						
WOODWORK						
PHYSICAL EDUCATION		C			Satisfactory work.	R.E.C.

TERM LETTER: 'A' Very Good. 'B' Good. 'C' Satisfactory. 'D' Weak. 'E' Very Weak.

REMARKS

Helpful and pleasant boy He works to the best of his ability.

E. White...............
Form Master.

Parent's Signature.........................

REMARKS

J.R............
Head Master.

Next Term begins on......... 3 SEP 1970

Unfortunately being on the small side I had the job of recording the weights and ear numbers. I started to shake from head to foot. They told me not to worry and they would explain it to me as they went along. Writing like a spider had crawled over the page, they never said a word it was just accepted, that was better than a million pounds to me, I really felt accepted.

The budget for school is first and foremost in the head's eyes, then keeping pupils at the school because they have pound signs over their heads. I have known a school take on a disruptive child who caused mayhem whichever class he was in, stopping people like myself from learning, just because of the pound signs. I am afraid that is false economy.

Also the failure of addressing the teacher shortages is not very professional for either the school or the authorities as their duty is to educate people, with no one accountable the situation can continue for years, which in this case it did, but it took a very shrewd move to take it out of the limelight.

With so many people behind the standard action needed to be taken. By reducing the level of standard in a low achieving class, makes them look as if they are improving, on paper, which was the only evidence the parents had, unless the parents took a close interest in their child; unfortunately I didn't come into this category.

Seven weeks holiday, heaven; clearing out the grain stores and barns ready for harvest. Cleaning out grain stores has to be thorough, making sure there is no trace of weevils; which are a very small mite and hard to see. You normally see the dust move with the infestation, which is easily treated with a powder, the best scenario is clean thoroughly and don't get infested.

Cleaning barns to store hay and straw is much easier but entails encounters with rats, and mice. Mice are no problem, but rats are another story. What makes a good ratting dog, a dog normally plays at killing until it is bitten, then you have a good ratter, unless you have rats that have made tunnels in the ground, this is another ball game. Filling the tunnels with water sounds easy, but a rat will stay just below the surface and put its snout and eyes just out of the water to see if there's danger, if so it retreats to find an air pocket or another escape.

Realistically I had to find an escape; I know now that children can suffer from depression. I was very lucky as my father would have seen this as weakness, that's if I could have been diagnosed, or it would been: pull yourself together. Doctors were viewed very differently in my school days; if you told your mother you had earache, a small bottle of olive oil would be pulled out of the cupboard poured onto a teaspoon and warmed over a gas ring and poured into your ear and finished of with a piece of cotton wool.

September soon arrived and going to school crying for several days only caused me grief. The strange experience of being invisible comes to mind. Luckily harvest continued to the middle of September, due to the wet August, so every afternoon I rushed home, and down the farm; no worries about tea, sandwiches were eaten later in the evening after the corn became too damp to combine.

The sandwiches and home-made cakes were out of this world, tea and orange juice until it came out of your ears. I clean forgot about school, but all good things come to an end, as the darker evenings were drawing in, the excitement of the farm reverted back to weekends only.

Rumours started at school about a trip to Austria early in the New Year. Knowing that this trip would be beyond my means I dismissed it from my mind. Some weeks later a flyer was being passed around for second and third years. I just took the flyer with no interest and on my return home I handed it over to my mother, who said, "Your father can see this when he comes home." To my amazement the weekend brought good news with my father wanting more information on the trip.

When I returned to school on the Monday I asked my form teacher for more information. She informed me that there would be an evening meeting for people who were interested for their child to take part. I took home an invitation for my parents to attend a meeting just after the Christmas break.

CESTREHAM COUNTY SECONDARY SCHOOL
CHESHAM

REPORT FOR THE TERM ENDING................ 18 DEC 1970

Form .....2 P.....

No. in Form.....2.7.....

Form Position.......-......

Conduct..... *Good*

Punctuality..... *Good*

Attendance..... *Good*

Subject	Set	Term Letter	Exam. %	Exam. Pos.	Comments	Master
English	5	B–	68	5	He always works hard.	V.S.
Mathematics		D	19	25	Has difficulty at times	
Religious Instruction		C	26	6	Tries this year	J.S.
Social Studies		C–	46	17=	Has found the work difficult, but has worked hard	J.E.W
History						
Geography		D	18	23/24	Generally works well	
French		D	28	11/27	Finds this subject difficult.	
Art		—				(RW)
Craft						
Music		A–			A very good 'treble' singing voice	GAD
General Science		D	32	18	He could do better	TRW.
Rural Science		C–	54	13/26	Usually shows interest	
Technical Drawing						
Metalwork		C+	68		Pleasing exam result	AB
Woodwork						
Physical Education		C–			Work is satisfactory	JMM.
DRAMA		B–			Very enthusiastic works well with others	PAS

TERM LETTER: 'A' Very Good. 'B' Good. 'C' Satisfactory. 'D' Weak. 'E' Very Weak.

REMARKS

Though he has difficulties in various subjects he is prepared to do his best at them.

.... Form Master.

Parent's Signature....

REMARKS

.... Head Master.

Next Term begins on....

Shrewd moves on the school's part to downgrade the standards, which certainly worked on the parents, but who would believe such a change: one A and two Bs. It definitely didn't boost my moral, because I live the lie.

The date for the parents' meeting for Austria was hurriedly decided on because of the great expenditure needed on the trip, as well as on warm clothing. The evening went very well and a timetable put in place for weekly payment, of £5.00 a week and the total cost of £45.00.

Two shopping trips were planned for the purchase of warm clothing, an all-in-one suit for the cold, goggles to stop glare from the snow, gloves, and a hat, boots would be supplied with skis on the day of arrival. With my father's methodical ways each Monday I took the five pounds into the headmaster who signed my payment card. I had never felt so good; my parents paying an enormous amount of money for the trip to Austria, in the Easter holidays.

Apprehensive of the flight was an under estimation on my part; I had never seen anything so big as a BOAC 1-11. We boarded the plane through the tail section and took up our seats as the teachers pointed to them. Fortunately I sat by the window even though there was not much to see due to it being a late flight. When we landed, a bus was waiting to transport us to the terminal where we collected our luggage, then off to find our coach which would transport us into Austria. I was shocked to see police with guns all over the airport; I suppose that's what you get for being a country boy.

We travelled on the coach for several hours as our destination was just outside Innsbruck in a small hotel which was built in traditional Austrian style. It had gone midnight when we arrived so we were ushered into our room and told we had an early start the next day. The next morning eruptions started as nobody had woken for breakfast.

A few raised voices started the ball rolling, and then we were marched down to breakfast. You could cut the atmosphere with a knife; we bolted down our breakfast as the coach was now waiting to take us for our ski fitting. The language barrier started to cause problems as we were taken to piste where a cable car was on its final working days before closure. After the descent we milled around waiting for our skis. Around midday panic and frantic phone calls were made to the tour operator who informed the teachers that we should have gone to Innsbruck were we would be introduced to our instructor, who would then oversee our ski fitting. Of course time was now running short so we ran back to the coach and into Innsbruck. Luckily we soon found the shop and with no more drama completed our fittings in record time.

On our return to the hotel time was in abundance before the evening meal, so with a free hand we started to explore the village. Children are allowed into cafés until 22.00 hours and alcohol is also served at these establishments; you can image by teatime one or two had tried the local beer and thrown up whilst having their meal. One tried to run to his room and threw up on the stairs, so after the first day we were under curfew.

The teachers were distraught with embarrassment and restrictions on money allowances were tightened up to ensure alcohol consumption would be less likely. One or two were restricted to the hotel premises only.

After such a catastrophic first day the second day wasn't much better. As we queued for the coach we lent our skis against the wall of the hotel, a freak gust of wind caught one pair of the skis, which then started a concertina effect, and as they moved along the wall, a pair of skis went through the window. We all scrabbled to pick up our skis as the teacher turned the corner. We were in more trouble but this time it was an accident and it took a lot of convincing.

When we finally arrived at piste the group was split into two, morning and afternoon, so the afternoon group had to entertain themselves, so we wondered around the area which consisted of two hotels and a leisure complex. We found this rather boring for three hours waiting to go skiing. Eventually we took our turn learning how to snow plough which is how you make a controlled stop, but there was a rumbling sound, we all stared up the mountain and the snow at the top was on the move. The instructor ordered us off piste, we didn't take much convincing. Before we were off, as we retreated, the rumbling stopped but we still carried on retreating from the piste, when we finally reached the bottom the instructor congratulated us on our quick thinking and that we were safe as the avalanche had come to rest in the valley.

That finished the skiing for the day, so the decision was taken to return to the hotel. The scenic route down the mountain was quite breath-taking with waterfalls frozen, with only the slightest trickle of water coming over the top and drizzling down the big ice block and as you looked across the valley, the chalets roofs covered with snow; if only I had a camera. We then dropped off the instructor in Innsbruck.

With the curfew still in place life in the evening was quite boring, but luckily enough the teachers had a change of heart due to the excitement on the piste with the avalanche, they decided to take us ten pin bowling in the next village which was only a short walk away. When we arrived, there were only two lanes and the skittles were raised and lowered on strings. Of course it didn't take us long to tangle the strings, so a young lady in national dress tried to untangle them. As she bent over her Charles hung out and boys being boys a comment was made and we were asked to leave and go back to the hotel. Of course they stayed to finish their game. On the way back the boys lit up cigarettes and congregated at the end of the village. As there was no street lighting they thought they were safe, but they forgot when you drop a cigarette to the ground it's like a star burst with embers spraying out; yes we were back on curfew.

Austria was such a clean country; everyday whilst

picking up our ski instructor we witnessed the streets of Innsbruck being washed down by lorries spraying jets of water in all directions, washing roads and pavements. Unfortunately Andy found a discarded bottle on the mountain.

Our curfew started to become tiresome so the boys decided that they would enjoy themselves at any cost. The coach dropped us off as normal and they made a b-line to the leisure complex. They started to consume alcohol, not in vast amounts, but enough. By twelve o'clock we had to make a move, as we walked passed the rear of the hotel a bottle lay in the gutter. Andy decided to take a swing at the bottle with his boot, on contact it shattered, a fragment of glass flew up and hit Andy across the upper eye lid, he lunged forward and grabbed a signpost and twisted around until he hit the ground. We ran and found a teacher, they rushed Andy to the hospital, and he received several sutures and had to refrain from skiing the rest of the trip.

A shopping trip was planned for the Friday, to allow us to buy presents for our families; I bought an ornament of a squirrel for my parents, and lent the rest of my money to a teacher as he had insufficient funds for his presents.

Later that evening a meeting was called where we received our certificates for passing specified movements on skis and a lecture on behaviour for the trip home. I unwittingly thought I was safe and the holiday had gone well without having to write spell, or add up but there was an unexpected element to the trip, for children to come back through customs they have to fill out a green form, listing their purchases. Luckily I had only bought an ornament, but how do you spell ornament and squirrel? I went cold with no one to ask; after the shock I just scrawled over the paper and hoped for the best. Luckily the customs were not looking for children that day and nothing was ever mentioned so I let sleeping dogs lie.

Conversation hardly ever existed with my parents, so escaping to the farm was quite easy; they never realised the extent of the damage they had caused. If I talked about the farmer, I would get remarks like: he's your hero. Whether this hurt him in a funny sort of way I will never know, as this comes under weakness.

Surprisingly we had to write an essay on our Austrian trip even though the trip was taken in our own time. I tackled the project to the best of my ability, but it didn't amount to much of a script, as most of the holiday consisted of misbehaviour and drunken stupor, which would have never gone down very well with the headmaster or the teachers. I am sure that was the final trip abroad for the school.

The main subject of the playground gossip was that more and more people were becoming discontented with the school meals; personally I found them quite good, but as I found out I was in the minority.

First and second years always had first sitting for school meals. The teachers had their own table

CESTREHAM COUNTY SECONDARY SCHOOL
CHESHAM

REPORT FOR THE TERM ENDING................16th July, 1971............

Form................2 Penn...............

No. in Form............26....

Form Position................................

Conduct............*Good*............

Punctuality............*Good*............

Attendance............*Good*............

Subject	Set	Term Letter	Exam. %	Exam. Pos.	Comments	Master
English	5	B	60	4	A pleasant, hard working boy	J.B.
Mathematics	4	C	33	14	Tries but finds it hard going	
Religious Instruction ...		c	19	14	Fairly satisfactory	
Social Studies		C-	87	15	He tries hard	
History						
Geography						
French		C-	16	20	He finds this subject hard going	KS
Art		c			Has made a good effort	
Craft						
Music		c.			Satisfactory work.	Pw
General Science		C-	27	16	Has progressed reasonably well	
Rural Science		C	40	17	Usually works with interest	
Technical Drawing						
Metalwork						
Woodwork		C+			Quite a pleasing beginner	
Physical Education		D+				
DRAMA.		B-			Takes others' ideas and develops them in an original way	

TERM LETTER: 'A' Very Good. 'B' Good. 'C' Satisfactory. 'D' Weak. 'E' Very Weak.

REMARKS

Though not the ablest of boys, Michael is a pleasant and helpful lad who will always try.

....
Form Master.

Parent's Signature................................

REMARKS

Has tried hard, and earned a creditable report.

....
Head Master.

Next Term begins on............2 SEP. 1971

set in one corner by the entrance. One person from each table was responsible for collecting the meals from the kitchen serving hatch and they also had to return soiled utensils. As normal I sat at my table and was eating my meal. One or two of the boys were feisty and nit-picking about the rice but I thought nothing of it, ate up and left the dinning room with the others. Around fifteen minutes later cheers rung out around the school and everybody started to make their way towards the dining room, as it could be viewed from the outside. Food was being thrown from all angles of the dining room; there was food on the windows, floor, and ceiling, total pandemonium. The cook walked out so that was the end of school meals for a very long time.

As I lived some distance from the school, packed lunches were the only alternative. I tried the fish and chip shop, but there was no variety and they were too expensive every day. The school cook took the matter very seriously and didn't want to return, so push came to shove, and school meals returned for first and second years only, but the head cook never returned.

"A pleasant hard working boy, and tries, but finds it hard going," will never secure me employment. The gaps in the report were teacher shortages or was it lack of funding, but with this scenario it could only end in tears. Normally a person that is not academic excels with hand skills, unfortunately

I will never get the chance to prove or disprove this point.

To help combat failing pupils like myself a thirty-minute spelling lesson was organised once a week. This was a catastrophic failure, as the teacher was not strong enough to keep order in the classroom. Pupils ridiculed him the whole of the lesson and we had threats of the cane, detention, and even reported to the deputy head but they just ridiculed him even more, because they knew he would only be showing his weakness to work colleagues, and no teacher can go through that humiliation.

People that cause trouble in classrooms and bring the class into disrepute never worry about getting on in life. The annoying part is they normally do get on in life whether it is honestly or not, but people like myself never have the chance.

The rural studies teacher very bravely asked for pupils' names that were interested in a week's visit to a rural study centre near Chalfont St Giles which would take place in the New Year. The paper was very soon filled with applicants. I asked my parents very gingerly and they soon agreed, so I put my name forth, and luckily I was accepted for the trip, a short list was made up and information passed out about clothing requirements; Wellingtons and duffle coats were the main items.

A new format for the school report which looks

Cestreham County Secondary School
Chesham, Bucks.

PUPIL'S NAME ~~████████~~ YEAR GROUP 3

LEARNING TO LIVE — REPORT FOR THE PERIOD ENDING December, 1971.

SUBJECT		% or GRADE	REMARKS	TEACHER
ART and CRAFT			Has been following a combined course	AW
MUSIC and DRAMA				
PHYSICAL EDUCATION		C	Satisfactory work.	REC
SOCIAL STUDIES		26% / 29/30	Michael, really must try harder - he is too easily distracted from his work	R.E.O.
ENGLISH		C+	Will do well if he makes the effort	MH
FRENCH		Exam 38%		
MATHEMATICS Set 4 out of 5		80% / 3rd/15	He is making good progress. Always does his best.	EW
SCIENCE	R. STUDIES	25.	He will do better when his powers of concentration improve.	Gy
	General Science	18%	Always tries hard and there has been some slight improvement	
TECHNOLOGY	T.D	30	Weak rather below standard	
	WW	45	Fair	

'A' Very Good. 'B' Good. 'C' Satisfactory. 'D' Weak. 'E' Very Weak.

FORM TEACHER
A satisfactory term generally. I would like him to try a little harder all round.

[signature]

HEADMASTER

[signature]

Parent's Signature

Next Term begins on 5th January, 1972.

better as they could mask some of the subjects; surely art and craft, music and drama are not linked? Teacher shortage springs to mind. Must try harder: it looks as if there is only one teacher who was paying attention for the last 2.5 years; she has the initials E W.

I believe that younger teachers of my school jumped to conclusions rather than made a study of who the trouble makers were. If you have a disruptive group in a class then the whole class is disrupted. Concentration during verbal confrontation is beyond most people, so looking up and blaming a particular person was very easy, because most of the class were looking up, and the first person they see, their card is marked.

Psychologists could have played a key role in this case but unfortunately there wasn't a strong enough person, or persons, to take the case to them. I will never know the truth, but over the years I have analysed many conversations which involved people mentioned in this story, so I am 99.9% sure that it would have caused embarrassment to the family, so I tragically have to suffer.

Our excursion to the rural studies centre soon rolled around. The journey only took half an hour by mini bus. When we turned off the main road to the centre, a beautiful leafy track lay forth which then opened up onto a tree-lined avenue. Set back into the woodland were three wooden structures, which consisted of dormitory, classroom, and a common room come dining room. The dormitory consisted of two lines of beds with a semi-enclosed room at the bottom for the teacher, and at the very end was the shower block and toilets.

After the unpacking ceremony a guided tour took place around the facilities and then inside for the timetable of the week's events, which included an off campus walk to a local college which specialises in agriculture, which sounded very interesting to me.

Funnily enough the evening actually flew past, with a main meal like your mum would make and a pudding you could die for, a real home from home treat, but that came to an abrupt halt as the teacher announced the field trip had been brought forward to the next day due to the weather forecast.

I retired to the dormitory worrying about making notes on the field trip. I knew I would have a harrowing night thinking of nothing else; in situations like this I never sleep, that is true to this day.

The sun started to rise in the sky and shone through windows of the dormitory, so it wouldn't be long before the torment and anxiety would be at full intensity. To escape the ridiculing from the gang, I would have to remember as much detail as possible.

After breakfast we returned to the dormitory for our Wellingtons, duffle coats, and the cause of my entire problem, the clipboard and pen. We set off across country towards the college. We hadn't been walking long when we felt spots of rain, the whole rescheduling of this field walk was to miss the rain, but we had passed the point of no return.

The heavens opened; who said there is no god, you cannot write on wet paper. It didn't take long before moans and groans started, the rain came down that hard we were soaked in minutes, Of course duffle coats soaked up water like a sponge, so the disciplined order soon went out of the window. We trudged across the road to the college entrance and as you looked down the quiet lane there was mud and puddles everywhere.

Extensive refurbishment had been running for several months, leaving all areas like a bomb site, building material everywhere; in the early seventies health and safety didn't play such a dominant role, with no cordoned off areas or any clue of definition so we walked into the bomb site.

John had decided to jump in every puddle he came across, the teacher was busy trying to keep us moving at a reasonable pace, when suddenly with a big splash John disappeared in front of our eyes. Seconds later he resurfaced; he had unwittingly jumped into a hole dug for a drain. With a gasp of air he shouted, our reaction being too slow he disappeared again. With no definition the hole could have been metres wide, so we gingerly moved forwards as sure-footed as possible ready to grab him when he popped up again. Wearing a duffle coat and Wellington boots wasn't helping the situation as they both retain water and would make him less buoyant. We managed to grab his shoulders when he broke surface again; a terrific weight as we dragged him to terra firma.

Luckily he didn't swallow any water as it resembled soup. We returned him to his feet and water cascaded from his clothing and he lent on my shoulder to empty his Wellington boots. He then walked to the college and arrangements were made for him to return to our dormitories.

If this incident took place today, an ambulance would have been called, health and safety informed, police notified, and a solicitor would have been appointed; the outcome of this fiasco decided the pupils were at fault for misbehaving.

The majority of the pupils continued the field trip around the agriculture college viewing a variety of animals and buildings; this did interest me, as farming was one of my career choices.

We trudged back to the rural studies centre where we showered and changed before returning to the classroom. John looked no worse for his incident at the college, then the teacher grasped the moment to reinforce his earlier statement on misbehaviour during the field trip, and the incident was due to pupils not walking as a group, or an orderly manner.

That evening they tried to relax in the common room talking about the day's events, with John taking most barracking about his star role as a magician which left me wondering whether the information I had gathered during the day in my head would be enough to save embarrassment the following day.

Another sleepless night worrying about school-work with the quotation, "School days are the best days of your life." I can honestly say that they were the most brutal days of my life, never knowing whether you would have verbal or physical abuse, owing to learning difficulties which were totally out of my control. Believe me, if I had control of this disability, I would take the better option.

As I tossed and turned in bed my attention was drawn to a moaning sound three beds to my left. Suddenly a silhouette appeared passing my bed in the direction of the toilets, gathering pace until they were running, then a thunderous crash and a bang.

Immediately the room was illuminated and a groaning sound from the teachers' quarters. We ran down to find Frank had tripped over the door threshold and threw up at the same time, leaving vomit up the wall and over the floor.

The teacher stomped around accusing us all of consuming too much fizzy pop and chocolate. We all denied the allegations but with the teacher blatantly ignoring our pleas he sent us back to bed.

The following morning the inquests reopened, and fizzy pop and chocolate appeared at the top of the list, with the blame firmly in our court, and the reputation of the school ruined. The pupil in question tried to put over his case, as he still felt unwell but he was blatantly ignored again.

The lessons resumed as normal after breakfast, but the atmosphere that was being radiated into the room considerably caused a lack of interest on everybody's part. The day dragged with very little being achieved.

A dramatic change came that evening with many other pupils starting to feel queasy and vomiting. The trip was abandoned the next day, with a virus being the diagnosis.

Most of us returned to school on the Monday, with very little being said about the outing. We filtered back into lessons with the experience firmly behind us. As normal my parents showed very little interest.

Suffering in silence does irreversible damage to a person's mind, as that person goes back into themselves and conversation dries up. The offenders are normally the first to notice this problem saying, "You don't tell us anything anymore," or they lose their temper, asking why, and then start having conversations with people, about you, in front of you. "He doesn't say much."

The whole scenario becomes a vicious circle.

The seven weeks' holiday I spent on the farm, away from the family, caused an inquisitive reaction with my parents, because we travelled to the cattle markets and slaughterhouses, where the animals are slaughtered in a different way because of religion, also to other farms to help worm cattle.

Cestreham County Secondary School
Chesham, Bucks.

PUPIL'S NAME ▨▨▨▨▨▨▨ **YEAR GROUP** 3

REPORT FOR THE PERIOD ENDING 19th July, 1972.

SUBJECT		% or GRADE	REMARKS	TEACHER
ART and CRAFT		B-	Must really concentrate / Continues to work well	Day / AB
MUSIC and DRAMA		C+	Some quite good work	PW.
PHYSICAL EDUCATION		G+	Satisfactory effort.	REC
SOCIAL STUDIES	SS.	2737 33	If he put as much effort into his work as he does into talking, he would improve greatly. Though he has begun to take his work more seriously over the past few weeks.	MUW
	Extra SS.	3	Has done some quite good work on his project.	MUW
ENGLISH	Group 4	C+	Usually makes a good effort.	MH
FRENCH				
MATHEMATICS	Set 4	71½% 4/14	Always does his best.	EW.
SCIENCE	Physics	36%	Agreat improvement, keep it up!	TRay
	Chemistry	23%	Tries, but finds the subject difficult	
	R. Studies.	45	A definite improvement on last time	
TECHNOLOGY	T.D.	18%	Finds this subject difficult.	
	W.W.	D	Little progress	

'A' Very Good.   'B' Good.   'C' Satisfactory.   'D' Weak.   'E' Very Weak.

FORM TEACHER Mr. Leith

Michael tries most of the time, and has made improvements.

HEADMASTER

Parent's Signature

Next Term begins on 5th September, 1972.

The farm created a vast learning curve, admittedly not the help in education I needed, but definately in life. I couldn't do enough for this man. He taught me how to drive tractors, reverse single axle trailers, and even a trailer with a steering axle. This fascination meant I never thought about crime or drugs; the temptation was never there.

On several occasions I really put myself through the mill, because of my enthusiasm. I would work from dawn till dusk to keep my mind off school, or any other threat; out of sight, out of mind, that's how I liked it.

I collapsed on these occasions with exhaustion; it always caught up with me at school. I used to complain of feeling ill before leaving for school and my mother would say, "You'll feel better when you get there." So thinking Mother knows best I would set off. By midmorning I would be staggering around having problems standing upright.

Convincing the school to let me go home without calling my parents was difficult, terrified of what reaction that would cause. I slowly but surely trudged towards home. On reaching our local shops I bumped into my mother, of cause there was a short court of enquiry, trying to convince her I couldn't walk anymore didn't sink in; with the reply, "I cannot carry you, so get home when you can," and she walked off.

Picking myself up to continue the last three hundred yards was agonizing, but there was no option. I had embarrassed my mother so much she didn't want to be seen with me, so totally alone I managed to crawl home.

Lying in bed on cold winters' nights listening to the wind and rain beating on the window, crying myself to sleep: how will I be able to earn money to live? My father had all ready told me that he would never employ me.

If only they could bury their pride and embarrassment and allow a statement to be drawn up; I would then receive all the help I need. People like my parents play into the hands of the council, without the statement you are just a normal pupil, which allows the council/school to leave you at the back of the class, still seeing a pound sign over your head. But the money helps their statistics: say 24 passes one miss, a very good result.

With the new term starting and new faces in the classroom, I met two boys that came from a farming background. We actually sat at the same table eating our sandwiches with one thing leading to another. Fred actually lived in a windmill, several miles away.

His father, a highly qualified aeronautical engineer, constructed new sails for the windmill, and renovated the whole structure. The grain store at the back contained a kitchen, living room, and bathroom; the lower and largest part of the mill contained the main bedroom.

During a cross-county run I managed to introduce Fred to my mother, we actually passed my front door whilst on the run, "legally" after having a quick drink and a few words my mother seemed to like him; wonders will never cease.

Fred was a latecomer to our class and I wondered if he would pick up on my absence from some lessons. He didn't suffer from learning difficulties. Luckily enough he never made any comments so our friendship would grow even though it would be a slow process.

After several weeks of knowing Fred he invited me to the windmill, which would take place on a Friday afternoon, we would catch the bus to the windmill and my father would pick me up later that evening. I gingerly put the idea to my parents who agreed. I knew that I would never be able to return the pleasantry because my parents would not permit such a thing; people very rarely stepped across the threshold in our house, even some relations didn't make it.

When my father picked me up, he wouldn't stop talking about the windmill, he had never spoken to me so much., I couldn't understand it; why show interest in me now? Of course I have never gained the art of conversation, "because children are seen and not heard" so then he started getting annoyed, but he had caused this problem.

I can imagine the scene; "Mick's been invited to the windmill on Friday by his best mate," and to carry this on, he would have to know more information, that's why he wanted to talk.

The point of no return had been reached with my education, and no remorse from my parents for failing to ensure I had the proper resources for my special needs, the only costs: TIME.

Cestreham County Secondary School
Chesham, Bucks.

PUPIL'S NAME ▬▬▬▬▬ YEAR GROUP 4

REPORT FOR THE PERIOD ENDING 21st December, 1972.

SUBJECT		% or GRADE	REMARKS	TEACHER
ART and CRAFT		D	A non-productive term	CR.
MUSIC and DRAMA				
PHYSICAL EDUCATION	Games		Satisfactory	REC
SOCIAL STUDIES	History Term Exam 17/21	D 34/1	A lack of ability and his difficulty with concentration have given him low marks	JBAR
	Geography	43	Is making limited progress but I feel that this will improve in later years	EHW
ENGLISH				
FRENCH		27%	I am sure he can improve on this	JE
MATHEMATICS	Set 4/4	73% 34/18	Always gives of his best.	GW.
SCIENCE	R. Studies	C+	Though academic work is limited he is always amenable, willing & reliable.	GW
TECHNOLOGY	Sa Practical	B	Can work well.	C. Ablett
	Prod. Sc	53	Always works well.	CAB

'A' Very Good.   'B' Good.   'C' Satisfactory.   'D' Weak.   'E' Very Weak.

FORM TEACHER Mr. Leith

Generally satisfactory, and sometimes better.
Improvement will always come to people who, like Michael, keep trying.

A. Leith

Parent's Signature

HEADMASTER

Next Term begins on 8 JAN 1973

Hurting the parents' pride and causing embarrassment is part and parcel of the child growing up. People with children take no notice as they have probably been through the same problems themselves; we are not robots and fully programmed on birth. It takes time and patience to educate your children and they are definitely nothing to be ashamed off.

Running up to the final year means that big decisions have to be made about which subjects to keep and which subjects to drop; I cannot make any sense of this practice as my educational ability is way below standard.

Pupils that are above standard can afford to drop subjects so they can concentrate on their specific and nominated subjects, but because I fall into the minority it's easier to leave me behind, knowing that there will be no reprisals because he signs his name at the bottom of every report, with no action taken.

On making the decision of which subjects to take I knew that I would come under fire from one party or another. Instead of contributing to a decision where everybody would be happy, they would criticize after making the decision myself; crazy world.

Unwittingly I was guided into another direction by a teacher that probably understood me and my disability, but could not openly say or put into writing the truth, so in his lessons we were asked to map out and dig a stop and catch base, for pole vaulting.

This snowballed into a stone age roundhouse, but with limited resources and pupils that thought it was a big game and after receiving a cut in the head by a flint, I lost interest.

All this activity comes under the heading school projects, which has no real meaning in a school report, especially as you don't gain a grade or any other results.

It's awfully lonely out there with no guidance from an adult or even adults that are not concerned about your education; these people must have no conscience or bad memories.

The choices I made were unachievable due to the teacher shortages; metal work and woodwork. Unsurprisingly I had to keep physical education, so really the choices were never there. My educational years where dictated: from day one I was destined to fail. Who in their right mind can be that cruel?

With the promise of two weeks of school with work experience most of the year was frantically running around trying to find relations or friends to send in a letter stating their business, so they could be released from school.

I made no attempt to find such a person. I knew the answer before I asked, even though they didn't mind about the farm; it is school time.

Exams were totally beyond my ability, knowing that I would come under some serious scrutiny from teachers and pupils, especially from the physical education department, as they think with their testosterone, and not their brain.

The physical education departmentt in the school was; look at me I'm beautiful, look at my muscles, and always ready to ridicule anybody that moves into their space; "I walked around the sand pit one dinner time and received three whacks with the slipper for playing in the pit, that's how they got off."

Bullying is a soul-destroying action especially when it's repeated everyday. For many months I'd been receiving a kick in the shin whilst changing classrooms. You can imagine fifty boys passing on the stairs, going up on the left, coming down on the right, with two flights of stairs, always when I was going up and changing with a certain class, I received a kick in the shin, but who is it, the person level with you, or the person just passed you, or the person coming up to you?

A brutal kick every time, with excruciating pain you shout and stop, but who is it? Everybody on the stairwell burst out laughing except you. After it has happened several times you develop a fear of the stairs, with big bruises on your shins, you have one hell of a job explaining how you received them.

Cestreham County Secondary School
Chesham, Bucks.

PUPIL'S NAME ████████   YEAR GROUP 5

LEARNING TO LIVE   REPORT FOR THE PERIOD ENDING 20th December, 1973

SUBJECT	% or GRADE		REMARKS	TEACHER
ART and CRAFT			Has worked hard and well on projects	Ay
MUSIC and DRAMA				
PHYSICAL EDUCATION	Games		Satisfactory	Rivoli
SOCIAL STUDIES	Group B1.	B.	A very keen and hard working member of the group	SHS
ENGLISH	Group D.	C.	Making satisfactory progress for the group.	SHS
FRENCH				
MATHEMATICS	Set 4	B+	A steady and most reliable person.	GW
SCIENCE	R. Studies	B	Michael has performed all tasks in a conscientious manner. Most willing.	Yhr
TECHNOLOGY	Gen Practical	A	Always helpful – a capable & reliable worker.	HS

'A' Very Good.   'B' Good.   'C' Satisfactory.   'D' Weak.   'E' Very Weak.

FORM TEACHER Mrs. Smith

An excellent report. I have found Michael to be a most helpful, mature boy.

Parent's Signature ████████

HEADMASTER

Courteous pupil.

Next Term begins on 7th January, 1974

Cestreham County Secondary School
Chesham, Bucks.

PUPIL'S NAME ██████████   YEAR GROUP 5

LEARNING TO LIVE   REPORT FOR THE PERIOD ENDING   18th July, 1974

SUBJECT	% or GRADE	REMARKS	TEACHER
ART and CRAFT		Has shown ability and tenacity in tackling many useful projects	*Ruf*
MUSIC and DRAMA			
PHYSICAL EDUCATION	Games	Satisfactory	*RGC.*
		Satisfactory	*Rhodes*
SOCIAL STUDIES	C	Keen reliable hardworking	*EHW*
ENGLISH			
FRENCH			
MATHEMATICS	Set 4	B+	Has always given of his best.	*EW*
SCIENCE	R. Studies.	B	As stated before, Michael has been most careful and displayed initiative in many manual activities.	*GW*
TECHNOLOGY	Pract Sc	A	Has been most helpful & has carried out some construction projects of an advanced nature very much to his credit. A Most reliable & conscientious student.	*APb*

'A' Very Good.   'B' Good.   'C' Satisfactory.   'D' Weak.   'E' Very Weak.

FORM TEACHER   MRS. SMITH

Michael has been one of the most helpful boys in the school. What he lacks in academic ability he makes up for in social attitude

HEADMASTER

A well deserved winner of the prize for service awarded by the Rotary Club

Parent's Signature

Next Term begins on   4th September, 1974

Chapter Five

The Final Straw

The only option I had left open to me was farming education, as I thought, but approaching my parents didn't lead to much response or help. They agreed to fund the clothing and I would fund the moped from money earned from the farm.

Working through the summer holidays on the farm was a fantastic relief, which helped me build confidence. Joe put everything into his farm and was a true professional and his teaching ability was beyond exception. I thought that I had made the right decision; I could walk on water.

The course entailed being resident five days a week, which didn't cause too many problems. The course started on the Sunday as there were animals to feed and milk. We were shown to our living quarters which looked like a giant chicken shed; small rooms, very clean and tidy, meals very good.

Monday morning 5am, waking up to alarm clocks and the thundering of feet passing my door brought home comforts to an abrupt end. The crew scheduled for milking were leaving the building;

the farm where I worked was arable and beef cattle, no early starts like this.

The new starters to the college were instructed to meet in the main reception area after breakfast; the tutors introduced themselves and gave a brief description of their departments and duties. The grand tour of the farm was uncomfortable and rushed due to it being the busiest time of the year for farming and students had their assigned jobs to be carried out.

Returning to the classroom for the last hour where we received details of the timetable for the following term and the field trip planned for the following day.

The facilities for the evening entertainment were very limited, so the newcomers could only stay on campus. The older students had cars and parents that would help with their financial shortfall, so you didn't see them for dust. My moped was only for travelling to the college and back, due to lack of funds for petrol.

After our field trip the following day we returned to the classroom, which shattered my confidence. The theory part of the course was far more intense than I thought, so from day two they ripped me apart in every sense of the word. When I returned home on the Friday I couldn't tell my parents or they would have ripped me apart. "If only they would give me an opportunity to talk to them", but I knew that would never come.

I had to force myself on the Sunday to return to college, and when I arrived back on campus you could see their eyes light up, knowing their target had returned. By Tuesday evening enough was enough; I packed my things knowing that round two would start at home.

I gingerly walked through the door and told them very carefully the problems I had. The old man bounced around the room several times then dragged me back to college,

We managed to arrange a meeting with a tutor, who told me that I had wasted his time and took up a place that another student could have taken; once again no one understands, no help, nothing. At this point I was asked to leave the room, my father and tutor carried on so I never knew the answers.

Suddenly my father came out of the office. I was then escorted to my room to make sure it was empty. Once I sat in the car the inquest started; everything was my fault, not his, when he could have sorted the problem ten years prior to me starting college and had me statemented at the age of six when he was first told about special needs. The summing up of the conversation was, "Don't think you are sitting on your arse with me keeping you, get out there and look for a job."

Chapter Six

Summing Up

Amazingly the school reports are showing a vast improvement until you take the time to read each statement, which mentions lack of ability, with only one teacher stating the facts consistently, perhaps the bureaucrats couldn't dissuade her as they do many others.

With the school's enormous catchments area the bureaucrats had to integrate people according to their ability, which is fine, but putting the lower achievers into categories and then lowering the standards, is covering up the problem.

Assess the problem and pass them over to a person that specializes in special needs. Dragging them through Secondary School with teacher shortages is a crime. If you have problems with English and Maths you obviously have problems elsewhere.

The understanding of the situation that teachers are trying to explain to you is the problem; if I receive one to one explanations I can do anything, groups of pupils together makes it hard to ask the question.

The only way I've managed to keep jobs is to adopt a positive attitude and reliability, which lead to an opportunity; leading a night shift that would run six months of the year. Of course I took the job. After the first month they approached me for a monthly report, as this would give the directors an insight into the shift. There was escape from this without causing some harm to myself, by the end of each month my guts had turned inside out.

For sure I went through humiliation that I would never have thought of. Every month I handed in my report, it was read while I sat there, and then the spelling lesson started by the works director; this happened every month I handed in a report. At the age of thirty-three I was asked to participate as a team in the writing of procedures for B.S.5750. I crumbled at the thought; I must say it was the biggest learning curve of my life.

Seminars had been organised to instruct the work force how to write the procedures correctly. I sat in the first seminar for the day with four others, after listening to the speech for an hour we were instructed to start writing. I just sat there with no idea how to start. I explained that I didn't understand the instruction, and apologized for being so dense.

So she could disparage me, she instructed me to sit alongside her, like a scolded child. I expected to hear sniggers but there were no evident noises. I didn't understand, so the young lady tried again. Nothing made sense, but so she could really stick the knife in, she opened up the statement to the rest of the room: does everybody else understand? The replies came back: No.

There was not one person in the room that understood the format or the instruction. I put myself through hell and back to actually admit I didn't understand, and the more intelligent people said nothing, until the young lady had ridiculed me.

With an immediate termination of the class we returned to work but still going though my mind was what haveI done. I will receive grief for totally demolishing the seminar. Unfortunately the young lady's contract was terminated.

Living with learning difficulties is like living with progressing disease; it stops you from achieving many goals. College courses are made more accessible now, but the budget still rules each and every department, so you will find your rights taken away. It's done very discreetly; I've come across examples like:

We have taken on a new student whose difficulties are far worse than yours, so the tutor will catch up with you when he can, but I will help as much as possible. Or unfortunately your special needs tutor has had to go part-time due to an illness in the family, so your rights has now been diverted to a third party, and your class tutor is now responsible for your special needs.

Schools offer extra help in the classroom hoping that you shy away from your child being statemented, with the councils encouraging this practice, because this gives them more control of the budget. Statements mean you're entitled to special needs help; no statement means they can take it away the next day.

The problem with school budgets is they are granted in parliament in the yearly budget in March, with it being dwindled down before it reaches the school i.e. last year the school went over budget, so that is taken off this year, then the teachers' pay rise, more depletion, so the amount that started out is no more.

In my case I came up as a budget saver repainting toilets, rebuilt a classroom wall and performed many other tasks, which saved their budget.

I have struggled all though my life and it is still a very lonely life. Hopefully telling this story will help with children reporting bullying and being statemented.

Closure

I would like to thank the counsellor who explained in great depth.

When things happen to children they cannot make an understanding of, they survive by putting these experiences in their memory in a way that make them safe. And some people find the only way to bring these memories forward is to find a counsellor who you can bond with and feel completely at ease with.

I personally feel that my problems have been with me for 42 years. Too long to allow my guard to be lowered to allow this person into my life, as this guard stops you from being hurt time after time.

For me to cope with everyday life I have found that there are many organisations out there that will write you a letter or give you advice free of charge, and admit that you have learning difficulties. You will be surprised at the reaction and how much more people will help you.

So the garage that keeps turning you away with the problem of your car, and the double glazing company that have made a right hash of your door fixing and will not return to rectify the problem, can be brought back into line and be accountable for their actions.

Some of the dates I have mentioned are approximations, but if this book helps one parent or child to receive the help "which is their right" I will then feel this book was well worth the sleepless nights and heartache over the several months of writing.

29